Basic
COMPOSTING

Basic
COMPOSTING

All the Skills and Tools You Need to Get Started

Eric Ebeling, editor

Carl Hursh,
environmental educator
and consultant

Patti Olenick,
soil scientist and consultant

Photographs by
Alan Wycheck

STACKPOLE
BOOKS

Copyright © 2003 by Stackpole Books

Published by
STACKPOLE BOOKS
5067 Ritter Road
Mechanicsburg, PA 17055
www.stackpolebooks.com

Printed in China

10 9 8 7 6 5 4 3 2 1

First edition

Photographs by Alan Wycheck
Cover design by Tracy Patterson

Library of Congress Cataloging-in-Publication Data
Basic composting / Eric Ebeling, editor.— 1st ed.
       p. cm.
    Includes bibliographical references (p.   ).
    ISBN 0-8117-2647-9
    1. Compost. 2. Organic fertilizers. I. Ebeling, Eric.
S661 .B38 2003
631.8'75—dc21

                                        2002015994

Contents

Acknowledgments

This book was a collaborative effort by so many talented people, and I hope I have managed to remember everyone who helped. My apologies to anyone I omitted.

My gratitude to: Alan Wycheck of Wycheck Photography in Harrisburg, Pennsylvania, whose skill behind the lens once again captured my vision for a book; Carl Hursh, whose composting skills are eclipsed perhaps only by his talents with homemade salsa; Patti Olenick, for shining her light through some dense material; Jina Padilla of Pennsylvania State Parks, whose keys unlocked a few important doors; Daniel Dindal, for the use of his classic illustration "inside" the common compost pile; Amy Wagner, for her sharp eye and even sharper wit; Tracy Patterson and Caroline Stover, for making this book look so good; Alison Abolins and Andy Goodwin, who donated their backyard as a shooting locale; Ed Abolins, problem-solver extraordinaire, for going that extra mile; Tim Maro, assistant manager and director of public works for the borough of Camp Hill, Pennsylvania, for making the time; and last, but far from least, my wife Andrea and son Alec, who somehow manage to teach me something new every day—even after all these years.

1

Introduction

You don't need a science degree or a shed full of sophisticated equipment to make quality compost. All you need is some know-how, a pile of organic materials, and a little bit of elbow grease. Nature does the rest.

The dark, rich soil covering the forest floor is a great example of this natural process in action. Fallen leaves blanket the dead limbs, plants, and other vegetation already on the ground. Over time, this mixture of materials breaks down into smaller and smaller pieces as millions of tiny organisms eat it, digest it, and convert it to waste. Think of these hungry decomposers as nature's cleanup crew.

Eventually this layer of decaying leaves and plants becomes a carpet of lush humus loaded with nutrients. New plants, shrubs, and trees take root and flourish in this rich material, and the natural cycle continues.

The process is much the same when you compost in your backyard.

The word "compost" comes from the Latin for "to put together," and that is quite literally what you have to do—put together the correct amounts of unwanted yard waste, food scraps, and other organic items; manipulate environmental factors to accelerate natural decomposition; and make compost for use in flower beds, gardens, lawns, or anywhere you would use fertilizer or mulch.

The basic composting processes detailed in this book require no highly advanced skills to complete successfully. Keep in mind that this book was not conceived to be a dense technical manual on the science behind composting. Rather, this book contains all of the essential information you need to know, presented clearly for ease of understanding.

Under proper conditions, yard waste, food scraps, and other refuse can be converted into nutrient-rich compost for use in gardens and flower beds.

ACT NATURALLY

Chances are, because you hold this book in your hand, you already have made the decision that composting is right for you. Just in case you have any doubts about the benefits of composting—from both a personal and a larger ecological standpoint—consider these facts:

Compost is less expensive than conventional fertilizer and mulch. Other than a few basic startup costs, the investment needed is a little time and a minimum of labor. Compare that with the price of a pound of fertilizer, and the savings are obvious.

Fresh compost has been called a gardener's best friend. Compost improves the texture of any kind of soil—silty, sandy, hard, loose—and allows it to hold more water or to drain more efficiently. It basically replenishes the "living" part of the soil to make it a healthy, productive environment so plant roots can grow and thrive.

The projects contained here—building your own composting bin and screener, for instance—require only common tools and a basic understanding of how to use them. You do not need to be a carpenter or a skilled handyman for these do-it-yourself suggestions.

Compost acts as a slow-release fertilizer, providing a wide range of nutrients, enzymes, and vitamins over time that plants need to stay healthy and flourish. Microorganisms in the compost allow these nutrients to be absorbed more readily into the plants. Most finished compost contains a pH level that is almost neutral—meaning it is neither too acidic nor too alkaline. A majority of plants respond well to soil with a neutral pH, and this can give your plants, shrubs, and lawn a more lush appearance. What's more, the natural properties of compost eliminate the need for harsh and expensive lawn chemicals that can adversely affect the environment.

Beneficial insects, earthworms, and other small creatures find compost to be an appealing habitat, and they can aid plant growth by creating underground passageways for air, water, and nutrients to get to plant roots. Experienced gardeners know that the presence of hearty earthworms is a true sign of healthy soil.

Used as mulch, fresh compost helps soil to retain moisture during dry periods, protects it from heat, and insulates plant roots when temperatures turn colder.

In addition to the benefits seen in the soil and throughout the garden, the process of composting effectively removes materials from your community's waste stream. It rescues and recycles waste that would otherwise be destined for disposal in the landfill. Environmental officials estimate that up to 20 percent of the trash collected by municipalities during an average year is made up of grass, leaves, and other backyard refuse that easily can be recycled.

This material invariably makes its way to a local or regional landfill, where it occupies valuable space needlessly. Composting, done properly, can eliminate nearly all yard waste from the municipal waste stream.

The best part of all is that composting is easy to do, and the compost you produce will be as good as or better than any sold at a garden center.

A layer of mulch made of compost will help keep the soil healthy, which in turn will allow plants to flourish.

2

Determining Your Needs

Before you build your first compost pile, you must determine your needs based on the amount of organic materials you regularly have available to add to the pile, the space you have for composting, and the degree of effort you are willing to put into the process. The person who lives in the country and the person who lives in an urban apartment have drastically different composting requirements that must be considered at the outset.

The amount of food scraps, yard waste, and other organic materials you generate will help you decide the type of bin most suited to your needs. Common sense dictates that you should use a larger bin if you have a lot of materials and a smaller one if you don't have as much. Composting can be done without the use of bins such as in a free-standing pile or below-ground pit.

Take Note
Keep in mind that local laws often prohibit open composting because it can attract pests, generate odors, and become unsightly.

Most commercial bins are designed to handle moderate amounts of materials generated by the average household. For example, a homeowner in a suburban neighborhood will have little problem maintaining a commercial bin with the lawn clippings, leaves, and food scraps typically generated over the course of a year.

People who have more land, a large number of leaf-producing trees, or bigger families that produce more food waste should consider composting on a larger scale.

The three-bin system detailed on page 29 is good for composting a bigger volume of materials in different stages; several smaller commercial bins used in tandem also will work well.

People who generate mostly food scraps and little or no yard waste, such as those who live in an apartment or urban setting, should consider composting on a small scale.

Commercial bins come in a number of shapes and sizes to accommodate the needs of many backyard composters.

A three-bin composting system like this one can handle a large amount of materials in different stages of decomposition.

JUST A MATTER OF TIME

It cannot be emphasized enough that compost will occur without your intervention over time, but your involvement makes the activity far more efficient, meaning more compost more quickly. Specific instructions on how to build and tend a pile properly begin on page 39.

Vermicomposting, also known as worm composting, is a great alternative to the conventional outdoor bin method; it requires minimal space and can be done indoors. This kind of composting uses specific worms to eat leftover food and paper scraps, which are then converted into a nutrient-rich fertilizer for houseplants or small window box gardens. Despite the stereotypical image that worms have, this composting method is clean, odor-free, and very efficient when done properly. Best yet, the worm bin requires little space and can fit under the sink or a corner of the basement. For detailed instructions on building and maintaining a worm composting bin, see section 10, beginning on page 75.

Worm composting is a clean, efficient alternative to more traditional methods of composting.

A backyard, side yard, or any small piece of level land covered in grass or dirt is a good spot to set up your outdoor compost bin.

Choose a flat, open location like this when setting up a compost bin.

When selecting a location for your bin, don't pick a sloped area because your bin might topple over when filled, or materials might start a gradual downward slide and become hard to manage.

Some liquid parts of compost will drain from the bottom into the ground, which provides the added benefit of attracting earthworms and other creatures to aid in the breakdown of materials. Don't place the bin on a concrete foundation or similar non-porous surface because it will inhibit decomposition.

Do not place the bin against any structures, such as your house or a shed. The moisture content and warmth of the compost may warp the wood, and insects might cause unwanted damage or other problems. Make sure the bin is at least 3 feet away from trees and large shrubs because too much nitrogen might run off and affect them.

The location you choose should be easily accessible; the bin will require some maintenance and upkeep, and you should keep the areas above it and in front of it clear of obstacles. If the bin will be in direct sunlight, the compost pile must be watered regularly so that it doesn't dry out, which will slow or stop the decomposition process. A shady area is preferable but not mandatory.

Consider how you use the area around the compost pile. Make sure the bin won't interfere with activities such as lawn mowing or outdoor recreation. Typically, an area adjacent to a garden is a good choice because it is a low-traffic area. Cut vegetation and old plants can be removed from the garden rows and added easily to the bin. Conversely, finished compost can be taken from the bin and used in the garden with little effort.

You should consider overall aesthetics as well. Place the bin in an area where it is pleasing to the eye or complements the landscape or look of the property. Your neighbors most likely will appreciate your efforts in this regard too. Many of the commercial bins on the market come in dark colors or earth tones and are designed to be unobtrusive in a backyard setting. The do-it-yourself bins explained beginning on page 19 should fit in nicely with most backyard settings.

Composting can be done in one of two basic styles: single-batch or continuous pile.

With single-batch composting, proper amounts of materials are added only once to form a pile and are maintained until the compost is finished. This is the most efficient form of composting and produces the quickest results, factoring in such variables as regular turning, watering, and general upkeep.

Combining materials into a large single batch is an efficient way to produce compost quickly.

When food scraps and the like are added regularly to a bin, the materials must be turned and agitated to promote decomposition.

This method is perfect for seasonal brush cutting and leaf raking, provided that excess materials from the earlier part of the year are stored for later use to keep the proper mix of browns and greens in balance. While all commercial bins work for single-batch composting, revolving drum bins and round tumbler bins are the best for this style; the materials inside the bin can be agitated and turned frequently with a minimum of effort to produce compost quickly.

Some experts claim they can use this method to convert raw organic matter into finished compost in as few as two weeks; results like that are not typical for the average backyard composter, though. A good rule of thumb: a correctly built and maintained pile can turn to usable compost within several months; a more laid-back approach—involving less hands-on turning and tending—can take up to a half a year.

The other style of composting—known as continuous—has no real ending point because it is perpetual by its very nature. With this method, food scraps and other materials are added to the pile as they become available, so the heap is, in effect, a constant work in progress. Stuff that you might currently grind up in the garbage disposal or chuck into the trash can help make some great compost.

For example, when you eat an orange or banana, place the rind in the bin; when a loaf of bread goes stale, throw the slices in; when you trim the hedges, load the debris onto the pile. Many people keep a small, sealable plastic bucket under the sink or in a corner of the refrigerator to save discarded scraps until enough has been collected to put in the bin; this eliminates the need for a trip to the bin after every meal or snack.

Because "fresh" materials are constantly added to the pile, only portions of the mound low in the bin will turn to fresh compost at any one time. The remainder will simply have to be given more time to decompose and filter down toward the ground, where it can be collected when finished. See page 48 for information about identifying finished compost.

3

Composting Equipment

GLOVES

Choose a thick pair of work or gardening gloves designed to resist punctures and tears. Many types of vegetation that can be composted are thorny or covered in bristles and should not be handled without protection. The gloves also give you added protection from scrapes and nicks during pruning and clipping, and they can make handling food scraps a more appealing exercise.

PITCHFORK

This is the perfect tool for adding piles of cut vegetation and branches to a compost bin. The pitchfork's tines also poke down into a pile to introduce more air into it. Make sure you pick a model with metal tines and a reinforced handle, because cheap versions are more likely to break under the rigors of composting.

AERATORS

Aerators come in many different styles and sizes, but they all are designed to accomplish the same goal: allowing fresh air to filter into the compost pile and aid in the breakdown of organic matter.

The most common types of aerators have long handles and resemble screws or butterfly clips. Three kinds are shown here. Each works well for composting.

The aerator is inserted forcefully down into the middle of a pile and then, depending on design, either rotated or yanked upward to mix compacted material and introduce air.

9

BUCKETS/CONTAINERS

Old metal tubs and bushel baskets are great for holding and transporting materials for composting, and they can be obtained inexpensively at flea markets and swap meets. Think about what you already have around the house to use, such as old laundry baskets or kitchen garbage cans.

PRUNING SHEARS

These are needed for trimming excess growth off of small plants and also for snipping larger stems, twigs, and fronds down to a more manageable size for composting.

WATERING CANS

A can that holds 2 gallons is a good choice for use in composting. The large capacity ensures that you have plenty of liquid to add to your pile when maintaining it. Regular buckets and similar containers also work well, although a garden hose attached to a water supply is fine too.

LOPPING SHEARS

These large-size shears are used to trim branches and underbrush before adding them to the compost pile. The shears also can be used to chop thicker pieces of vegetation into smaller bits for the composter.

10

HEDGE CLIPPERS

These serve the same basic function as the lopping shears, except they are designed to cut thinner branches. The clippers can slice through material quickly because of the large cutting surface on the scissor blades, so they can make short work of longer pieces of plants, bushes, and trees.

SCREENER

This is used to separate large chunks of material that hasn't yet decomposed from the smaller, rich pieces of finished compost. See page 49 for detailed plans on building a screener.

FLAT SHOVEL OR TAPERED SPADE

This serves a number of composting purposes, including shuttling material from one spot to another, applying bulk compost to a screen for filtering, and transferring finished compost to the garden or flower bed.

KITCHEN SHEARS/KNIFE

Use these to cut food scraps into smaller bits when adding material to a traditional compost bin or a worm composting bin.

WHEELBARROW

Helpful for transporting large quantities of organic matter to the compost bin and for holding finished compost during application to lawns and gardens.

4

What to Compost

Now that you have selected a location, you need to know the kinds of organic material you should—and should not—add to your compost pile.

It's important to remember that efficient composting occurs when millions of microscopic organisms such as bacteria and fungi take up residence in your compost pile, continuously devour it, and digest it to produce rich material. Additionally, larger creatures such as worms and insects arrive to speed the process along. Like all living things, these organisms need a "balanced diet," water, and air to sustain them, and it's up to you to provide these favorable conditions so they can perform their natural role.

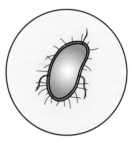

Diet

A balanced diet for these tiny creatures, known as microbes, is carbon and nitrogen and is provided when you add yard waste, food scraps, and other organic refuse to your compost pile.

For our purposes in composting, materials containing high amounts of carbon are considered "browns," and materials containing high amounts of nitrogen are considered "greens."

High Carbon = **browns**

High Nitrogen = **greens**

Browns are sugar-rich food sources that provide energy through carbon so the organisms can break down the organic material. The most common browns you will find are dried leaves, twigs, newspaper, straw, sawdust, and napkins and other paper supplies.

Greens provide protein sources to the organisms through nitrogen. The most common of these high-protein materials are grass clippings, kitchen food scraps, yard trimmings, and any other green plant debris.

FROM THE EXPERTS

To ensure that you have enough browns and greens to add to your compost pile as needed, store excess materials for use later, when they may be scarce.

To be efficient decomposers, microbes need a supply of food with a proper carbon to nitrogen ratio. This stimulates the microbes to reproduce, consume, and digest the organic materials in the pile, converting it over time into compost.

As they eat, the organisms generate a large amount of heat, which raises the temperature of the pile and speeds up decomposition. On cool mornings, you might even see steam rising from the heap.

The easiest way to achieve the proper ratio is to add two parts green materials to one part brown—regardless of the size of the "part." For instance, you could use a bucket or garbage bag as your gauge: Just make sure that for every bucket or garbage bag full of browns you toss onto your pile, you add two buckets or bagfuls of greens.

By following this simple rule of thumb, you will create a pile thriving with hungry microorganisms that will produce compost. Remember, organic material will turn to compost over time regardless of proportion, but results might not be seen for upwards of a year or more. For a slightly more technical approach to determining the carbon to nitrogen ratio, see the chart on the next page.

Microbes thrive best when their food source provides a carbon to nitrogen ratio (expressed as C:N) between 15:1 and 30:1—meaning that for every 15 to 30 parts of carbon, 1 part of nitrogen must be added to the pile. The ratio of carbon to nitrogen is a chemical one and is not based on volume; you do not need 30 times more brown materials than green.

To determine the carbon to nitrogen ratio, add materials to the pile in equal amounts. Then, add up the carbon for all of the materials in the pile and divide by the number of materials added.

Carbon–Nitrogen Ratio

Carbon sources (estimated):		Nitrogen sources (estimated):	
Bark	100–130:1	Alfalfa	13:1
Cardboard, shredded	200–500:1	Clover	23:1
Coffee grounds	20:1	Food waste	15–25:1
Fruit waste	35:1	Garden waste	20–60:1
Leaves, fresh	40–80:1	Grass clippings	15–25:1
Newspaper, shredded	150–200:1	Hay	25:1
Peanut shells	35:1	Manure, cow	20:1
Peat moss	30–65:1	Manure, hog	5–7:1
Pine needles	250:1	Manure, poultry	5–10:1
Sawdust	100–230:1	Meal, blood	3–4:1
Straw	50–100:1	Meal, bone	3–4:1
Wood chips	200–700:1	Vegetable peels	13–25:1

Compiled by Thomas Becker, Penn State agricultural extension agent, York County, Pennsylvania

This will give you the carbon to nitrogen ratio. For example, if three materials—food scraps, leaves, and grass clippings—were added to the compost pile in equal amounts, you would calculate the carbon content of each type of material; in this case, roughly 15, 60, 15. Add those three numbers together, for a total of 90. Divide that total by the number of different materials you added—in this case, three—and you end up with a ratio of 30:1, which is within the acceptable range.

Throughout many regions of the United States greens are plentiful during the spring and summer growing seasons, while browns are more difficult to find. In the fall and winter, the opposite is true: Browns such as falling leaves and dead garden plants are common, while fresh plant growth is not.

You can place the materials separately in bins or enclosures until you are ready to build your compost pile. Alternatively, you can simply cover the yard waste with a tarp until it is needed.

Many local municipalities have begun large-scale operations that collect leaves and yard waste from residents and turn it into beneficial compost using long windrows of material. You should use caution when applying this type of compost to tender plants and seeds because the makeup of the compost cannot be known with certainty.

Compost can be obtained inexpensively—even free—from many local municipalities that encourage yard waste recycling, curbside leaf pickups, and other environmental initiatives.

What to Compost

Food scraps (rich in nitrogen)

Perhaps the trickiest part of gathering food scraps for composting is modifying your behavior. Instead of putting fruit rinds and other leftovers down the garbage disposal or in the trash can, remember to throw them into your compost bin. Many who compost use a container such as a plastic tub with a lid to hold food scraps until enough collects for a trip out to the bin. You can store the container in a corner under the sink or on a shelf in the refrigerator, which will retard decomposition and prevent rank odors from developing.

Apples	Buckwheat hulls	Pears
Artichokes	Cabbage	Pineapples
Asparagus	Carrots	Potatoes
Bananas (fruit and peel)	Celery	Rice
Beans	Cucumbers	Squash
Beets	Grapes	Tea leaves
Blackberries	Lettuce	Tomatoes
Bread	Melons	Turnips
Broccoli	Oats and oatmeal	Zucchini
Brussels sprouts	Onions	

Other nitrogen sources

Alfalfa	Feathers	Humus or soil
Blood meal	Garden waste	Manure
Bone meal	Grass clippings	Seaweed
Clover	Hair	Sod
Commercial fertilizer	Hay	Vegetable peels
Compost, finished	Hops (used)	

Carbon sources

Bark	Leaves	Rope
Cardboard	Mushroom compost	Sawdust (from non-treated wood)
Coffee grounds	Newspaper	Straw
Corn cobs/stalks	Paper	String
Dried flowers	Peanut shells	Tea bags
Dryer lint	Peat moss	Wood chips
Dust	Pine chips	Wool or cotton scraps
Egg shells	Pine needles	
Felt	Plant prunings	

Bad Ingredients

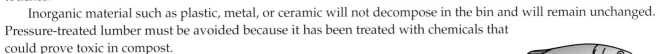

Do not compost the following items, because they can interfere with decomposition, create noxious odors, or attract pests to the pile:

Meats, bones, fish, and any food containing milk, eggs, and oils can produce very unpleasant odors in the compost pile and attract animals looking for a meal. Rotten meat may produce bacteria that can pose a health hazard.

Pet feces (cat, dog, bird) can make compost toxic to handle and must be avoided. Local municipal ordinances often prohibit its use as well. Manure, the waste product of farm animals such as cows, pigs, poultry, and horses, can be added in limited amounts to your compost pile to increase the nitrogen content if too many "browns" are present. Too much manure, though, can raise nitrogen levels above the proper ratio.

Do not add plant material that has been treated with herbicides or pesticides. Certain toxic chemicals might withstand the composting process and stay active in the finished compost, killing off or tainting vegetation it touches.

Inorganic material such as plastic, metal, or ceramic will not decompose in the bin and will remain unchanged. Pressure-treated lumber must be avoided because it has been treated with chemicals that could prove toxic in compost.

Do not add lime to a pile to try to balance pH levels, as it might cause the release of ammonia gas during decomposition. This gas smells unpleasant and can rob the pile of needed nitrogen. Finished compost routinely has a pH level that is neutral, meaning it is neither too acidic nor too alkaline.

Avoid adding diseased plants and leaves to a compost pile, because the disease could be spread later when compost is applied. In the same vein, do not add persistent weeds such as poison ivy, bindweed, quackgrass, and other types that spread easily and are tough to control. Although the composting process might kill off weed seeds, even a few survivors will mean headaches for a newly seeded lawn or vegetable garden.

Undesirables

Bones	Fish	Milk
Butter	Lard	Oils
Charcoal/coal	Lime	Peanut butter
Cheese	Magazines (inks, dyes)	Pressure-treated wood
Chicken	Margarine	Sour cream
Diseased plants	Mayonnaise	Vacuum bags and dust
Dog/cat feces	Meat of any kind	Yogurt

Water

The organisms that live in the compost pile require water for survival. It is important to keep the pile damp continuously; moisture content between 40 and 60 percent will ensure that the organisms flourish.

You can check the moisture content with a simple test. Take a handful of compost and squeeze it. It should feel like a wrung-out sponge. If it feels dry or powdery, you need to add water to the pile because the organisms will have a difficult time surviving. If a steady trickle of water flows when the material is squeezed, the pile is too moist. You should add dry materials such as leaves, paper, or sawdust to absorb the excess moisture. Too much water can cause the pile to stagnate and produce unpleasant odors.

Air

The compost pile needs ventilation throughout it to provide organisms with air, otherwise they will fail to reproduce and die. Decomposition that occurs in the presence of a rich source of air is called "aerobic"—just like the gym workouts designed to get oxygen flowing through the body. Aerobic decomposition is very clean and efficient, and it produces results with little or no odor.

On the other hand, anaerobic decomposition occurs when air is prevented from reaching the organic materials. This airless environment allows different kinds of bacteria to thrive, organisms that can cause foul-smelling gases to emanate from the pile. The anaerobic process is slow, and the resulting material is dense, wet, slimy, and harsh on the nose. The nasty muck that rests on the very bottom of a marsh or a bog is the product of this kind of decomposition.

Turning the pile with a pitchfork or shovel or poking it with an aerating device will keep air flowing and keep beneficial organisms happy. Techniques for turning and aerating the pile are included in section 6.

5

Bins

DO-IT-YOURSELF BINS

The Pile

Because composting occurs as a matter of course in nature, no special bins or enclosures are absolutely required for you to successfully compost.

The most basic of all composting techniques is called the "mound" or "heap" approach, and like it sounds, you simply pile up greens and browns until you have a large stack. However, these free-standing heaps can be unsightly and can attract a variety of vermin because they are unprotected; local ordinances often prohibit the presence of this kind of pile, so be sure to check the laws in your area before you build one.

Better still, construct a sturdy bin yourself like the one shown, or buy an efficient commercial bin.

Garbage Can Bin

This is among the easiest and most inexpensive of all composting bins you can make.

Choose the plastic type commonly sold in department or home improvement stores; make sure it has a lid that can be firmly attached to keep pests out. A plastic can is preferable to galvanized metal; numerous ventilation holes must be drilled through the sides, and plastic is much easier to pierce than metal.

These bins are sturdy, weather resistant, and will last indefinitely.

You can easily turn material loaded into this bin with a shovel or pitchfork, or you can mix the waste by tilting the bin on an angle and jostling or rolling it. This is a good bin for a household that produces a relatively small amount of food waste and yard debris.

Materials and tools

- ❏ Large rubber garbage can with lid
- ❏ Drill, with a $^1/_2$-inch bit

Drill $^1/_2$-inch ventilation holes at intervals of about 5 or 6 inches around the top section of the can. Continue by drilling holes down the sides of the can at regular intervals. Finish the project by drilling about six holes in the bottom of the can for drainage. Without these holes, excess water inside might become stagnant and produce foul odors.

Concrete Block Bin

Concrete blocks, also called cinder blocks, can be used to make a durable bin that will withstand the elements and last a long time. Arranging the blocks into the correct formation takes just a matter of minutes, but they are heavy and require some muscle to maneuver them into place. When finished, this bin provides an ample area for compost protected by walls on three sides, with an open top for access to the pile. If you need additional chambers for composting, simply build on to one of the two parallel walls.

Take Note

As with all compost bins, children should not be permitted to play on or around the concrete block bin to avoid the risk of injury.

The construction plans call for thirty-seven blocks that measure 8 inches by 16 inches; they can be found at home improvement stores, garden centers, and at local recycling or reuse centers. This is a good bin for a household that produces a moderate amount of organic material.

Materials and tools

☐ 37 8-inch x 16-inch concrete blocks with two or three center holes

☐ Work gloves, optional

21

Concrete Block Bin

1. Select a suitable site for the compost bin that is level, preferably located in a partially shaded area that is close to your garden. The space required for the bin is dependent upon the layout of the first course of blocks. A bin that is four blocks wide and three blocks deep requires an area of about 64 inches by 56 inches.

2. Build the rear wall first. Place four blocks end to end, arranged with the holes facing up. Use care to avoid pinching your fingers or hands.

3. Lay three blocks for the left wall starting from the left face of the rear wall.

4. Lay three blocks for the right wall starting from the right face of the rear wall.

  The blocks will form a U shape when viewed from above.

5. The second row is composed of ten blocks placed on top of the first and turned so the middle holes face sideways. These holes will provide ventilation to the compost pile. Set the blocks in place, making sure they are even with the row beneath and are butted firmly against each other end to end.

  The third course will consist of nine blocks.

6. Start with the left rear corner and lay the first block along the left side wall with the holes facing up. Place the block across the joint lines of the second-course blocks, as it will help "tie" them together and give them more stability.

7. Add two more blocks to the left wall, place three blocks across the rear wall, and place three blocks on the right wall to complete the third course.

There will be a gap of half a block at the front of each of the side walls.

8. Starting with the left rear corner, lay the first block of the fourth course on the rear wall across the joint line of the third row of blocks.

9. Lay three more blocks across the rear wall. Lay two blocks atop each of the side walls and against the rear wall blocks to complete the project. This final course of eight blocks will leave another gap of a half block above the third-course blocks.

10. The corners should fit together as shown.

11. The height of the enclosure depends on the number of courses of blocks desired. Four rows of concrete blocks will create a bin with adequate space for a large compost pile. Walls that exceed five courses in height should be stabilized with mortar between each course or metal bars along the outside walls.

When you finish putting the blocks in place, apply downward pressure to the walls to test them for stability.

The bin is now ready to accept materials for composting.

Wire Composting Bin

This is an easy and inexpensive bin that you can set up with just a few materials and very little time. Everything you need to build this bin can be found at a home improvement center or lawn and garden store.

Wire mesh material such as hardware cloth, chicken wire, or metal fencing will work well for building this kind of bin. A medium-gauge mesh is recommended: it provides greater stability than lighter materials, and it is more flexible and easier to work with than heavy-gauge metal. Plastic fencing, also called snow fencing, can be used as well, although it may need additional support from metal or wooden stakes.

The open mesh allows air to flow freely in and out of the compost pile, providing the oxygen needed for proper decomposition. This bin is very lightweight, so it can be pulled up and moved to another location if needed; this technique also works when you want to thoroughly turn the whole pile or harvest finished compost from the bottom layer. Just move the bin and use a shovel or pitchfork to mix and transfer the unfinished material to the new location, then collect the mature compost from the bottom.

Additionally, this kind of wire bin is perfect to use as a holding container for excess brush and yard waste that you would like to save from season to season.

Because the sides of the bin are wide open, moisture evaporates rapidly from wire composting bins. Make sure to water the pile regularly so the pile doesn't dry out, which will slow down the composting process. This is a good bin for a household that produces a moderate amount of organic material.

Materials

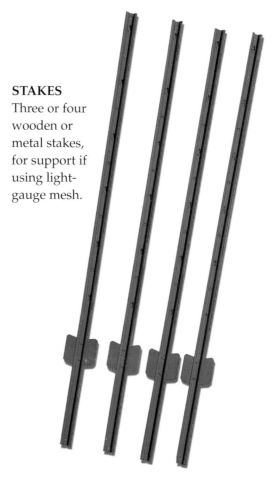

WIRE MESH
You'll need 10 feet of 36-inch-wide, medium-gauge, $1/2$-inch mesh. Plastic fencing can be substituted.

STAKES
Three or four wooden or metal stakes, for support if using light-gauge mesh.

WIRE
Three pieces of sturdy wire for use as ties, each 4 inches long.

Tools

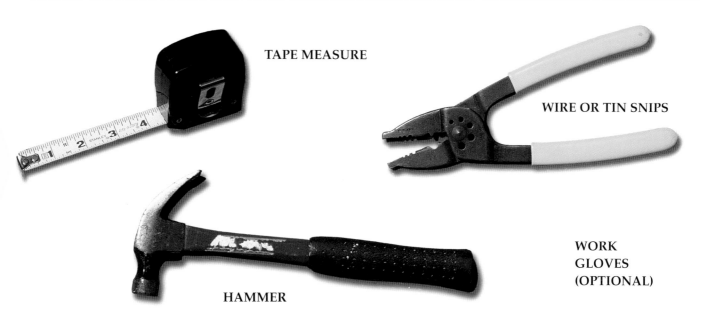

TAPE MEASURE

WIRE OR TIN SNIPS

HAMMER

WORK GLOVES (OPTIONAL)

Wire Composting Bin

1. Unroll the mesh, bending it back on itself if needed to eliminate curvature.

2. Use a tape measure and mark off a 10-foot-long piece.

Cut that section off with wire cutters or snips. Keep in mind that the mesh will be sharp when cut, so

handle carefully. It's a good idea at this point to bend sharp pieces of wire back so they don't pose a danger.

3. Set the section of wire up on its edge in the spot where the bin will be used.

4. Form the wire into a circle so both ends overlap slightly.

5. Use a wire tie to secure the two edges of the mesh at the top.

6. Repeat in the middle and at the bottom.

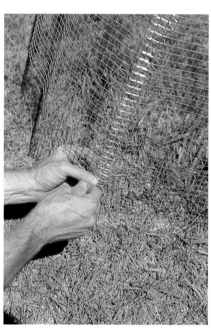

7. Depending on the gauge of the metal wire used in the fencing material, stakes might be needed at this point for additional support. Even if the mesh seems strong, it's still a good idea to reinforce the sides of the bin to eliminate headaches caused by a collapse later.

8. Simply place a stake inside the bin, close to the fencing, and hammer it firmly into the ground. Repeat using a four-corner approach until all of the stakes are used. Make sure to position each stake against the wire mesh to tighten it so that the sides do not sag.

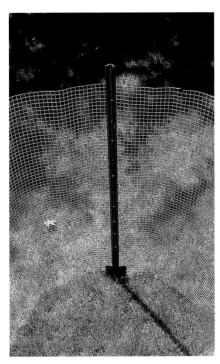

9. Check the fencing for any sharp or ragged edges that pose a risk of injury. Bend back or snip any sharp edges that you find.

10. You are now ready to fill it with materials for compost.

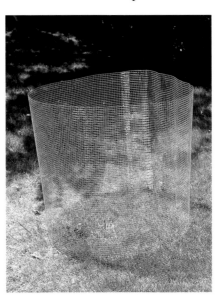

As an alternative, you can use a 10-foot section of rigid plastic material to form a bin. You must drill holes where the two edges join and fasten them with wire ties or nuts and bolts. Additionally, a few $1/2$-inch air holes should be drilled through the solid sides of the plastic to provide ventilation.

Three-bin Compost System

This is one of the largest kinds of bins. The three-bin design provides ample room for active composting, as well as space to store excess yard wastes. It is composed of ten wooden pallets, the sturdy type used for shipping and warehousing goods, which generally measure 42 inches by 48 inches.

These pallets are aligned and wired together to form three distinct composting chambers, each with a single front pallet that helps keep compost from spilling out.

They are often given away or sold inexpensively by warehouses, distribution centers, and the like—any place where merchandise, supplies, or equipment is delivered and stored. Make sure you choose pallets that are roughly the same size. A difference of a few inches in length or width won't interfere with construction, but anything more significant than that should be avoided.

Take Note

When selecting pallets, make sure they are in satisfactory condition. A few broken or worn-out boards here and there will not present a problem, but you should avoid pallets with a large number of missing slats or that contain rotten wood.

One person can build this bin system on his own, although a helper can be an asset when moving and securing the pallets during construction. This kind of bin is suitable for use by a household that produces large quantities of organic material.

Materials

PALLETS
Find ten shipping pallets ("skids"), approximately 42 inches by 48 inches.

WIRE
You'll need 40 feet of 12- or 14-gauge three-strand house wiring. Baling wire will work as well.

Tools

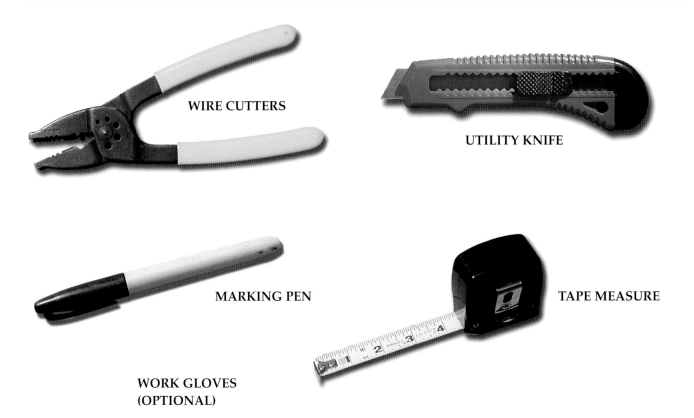

WIRE CUTTERS

UTILITY KNIFE

MARKING PEN

TAPE MEASURE

WORK GLOVES (OPTIONAL)

Three-bin Compost System

1. Select a suitable site for the compost bins that is level and preferably located in a partially shaded area that is close to your garden.

Determine the space needed for the "footprint" of the pallet bin system. It will encompass a rectangular area of approximately 4 feet by 12 feet, depending on the size of the pallets you use.

2. Measure, mark, and cut the wiring into ten 4-foot sections.

3. Strip the outer insulating plastic sheath from the wiring by cutting along the length of the sheathing with a utility knife.

4. Separate the plastic from the three wires inside. The black and white plastic-coated wires will serve as giant "twist ties" for connecting the pallets.

5. Set aside the third wire, made of copper, for other uses. It will not be used in this project.

Keep in mind the basic design of this three-bin system: Two four-pallet enclosures will sit at opposite ends of the space you have chosen for the bin. The area between them will be enclosed with pallets added at the back and front, thus completing a center enclosure.

6. Most pallets are not perfectly square. Determine the longest edges of two pallets and place them at right angles to each another with their long edges on the ground.

31

7. From the outside of the corner formed by the two pallets, thread one of the 4-foot pieces of wire through the top portion of each of the pallets and twist until tight to secure the upper corner.

8. Repeat on the bottom corner. Always work from the outside of the bin when twisting the wires to secure the corners.

9. Add a third pallet to continue the construction of the bin. Maintain right angles between each of the pallets as they are set in place.

10. Secure the upper and lower corners with wire ties.

11. Add a fourth pallet to complete the four-pallet enclosure and secure with the wire ties. This single unit can be used as a free-standing composting bin on its own at this point.

12. To continue building the three-bin enclosure, place a fifth pallet against the right rear corner of the left side enclosure.

13. Secure at the top and bottom corners by threading the wire ties through the pallets and twisting until tight. This pallet will serve as the rear divider between the two four-pallet enclosures.

14. Begin construction of the other four-pallet enclosure by placing a sixth pallet at a right angle to the center rear divider.

15. Secure the top and bottom of the corner with wire ties.

16. Add a seventh pallet at a right angle to the sixth pallet to form the rear side of the other enclosure.

The three pallets that make up the rear wall of the bin system should be aligned as straight as possible.

17. Secure in place with two ties at the top and bottom.

18. Add and secure an eighth and ninth pallet to complete the enclosure.

The remaining space for the tenth pallet is across the front of the center bin. Access to this space can be left open to make adding compost material easier. It can then be enclosed with the pallet as the materials accumulate.

FROM THE EXPERTS

For very fast composting, add material to the first bin and allow it to heat up and decompose for three to five days. After that, turn it into the middle bin and allow it to decompose there for four to seven days. At the same time, add new material to the first bin. Transfer the material from the middle bin to the last bin when it has turned into finished compost.

A wide variety of prefabricated composting bins can be purchased for backyard use. While each kind of bin may differ in appearance and use, all of them are designed to help you compost efficiently. You can find a bin to suit your needs in most home improvement outlets, garden supply stores, or on the Internet.

Generally these bins are strong and easy to assemble, can hold a 3-square-foot pile of material, and are designed to promote moderate to fast composting. Weather-resistant, these bins are virtually indestructible and will last indefinitely.

Most commercial bins are made of black or dark green plastic, which absorbs and retains heat generated by sunlight. The dark color and typically basic design make these bins fairly inconspicuous and less obtrusive than some homemade bins, so you should keep this in mind when making your selection. Their sturdy lids keep away pests when in place and when removed provide easy access for adding new material and turning the pile.

Numerous slits and holes throughout the bin allow rainwater to flow into the bin and permit good ventilation for the entire pile. These slits and holes are small enough to prevent rodents and other pests from entering the bin. Because excess moisture from the pile needs to drain off, these bins typically do not have bottoms.

The three main types of commercial compost units are enclosed bins, spherical—or ball—bins, and tumbler bins.

Bins

These sturdy yet lightweight plastic bins are the most common types available. The body styles of these are typically square and cylindrical. Both shapes work equally well for composting.

Turning compost with a pitchfork or shovel can be tricky in one of these bins because the shape can inhibit access.

Instead, consider using an aerator to punch down and twist into the pile periodically to mix materials and introduce more air.

Select the one that is most visually pleasing to you and that meets your space needs.

A nice feature on many of these bins is a sliding door at the bottom that provides access to finished compost without having to remove material on the top of the pile.

Many also feature a sliding lock mechanism that keeps the lid secured against pests and the wind.

Estimated price: less than $100.

Spherical Bins

This round or octagonal plastic bin is designed to be rolled on the ground to mix materials placed inside. This eliminates the need to turn the contents of the bin with a shovel or pitchfork and promotes speedy decomposition.

Materials are added through a hatch that can be closed and locked into place.

A number of air holes dotting the bin provide ventilation for the pile.

Keep in mind that bins loaded with material can become heavy and somewhat difficult to roll.

Estimated price: about $100.

Tumbler Bins

This type of bin features a rolling drum that is filled with material and turned by hand to speed up the composting process. Depending on the bin's design, the drum is either attached to a metal shaft and hand crank or sits on a system of rollers. The drum can be spun by hand with little effort even when nearly full, thanks to the energy-efficient design.

Organic ingredients are added through a hatch on the side of the bin, which is locked in place when not in use.

Air holes on the sides of the drum provide ventilation.

When materials need to be mixed, a quick spin of the drum sets the unit in motion much like a clothes dryer, tumbling and agitating the contents without the need for a pitchfork or shovel. The composting process can occur quickly, in a matter of weeks, in this kind of bin.

Estimated price: more than $100, and significantly more for larger size units.

Building the Compost Pile

If you use the single-batch method to build and maintain a pile during the warm seasons, you can expect to have usable compost within a few months. Composting happens quickly when air temperatures are warm, above 60 degrees or so. Very cold temperatures, such as those experienced in the northern United States during winter, will slow decomposition to a standstill until warm weather returns.

Anatomy of a Layered Pile

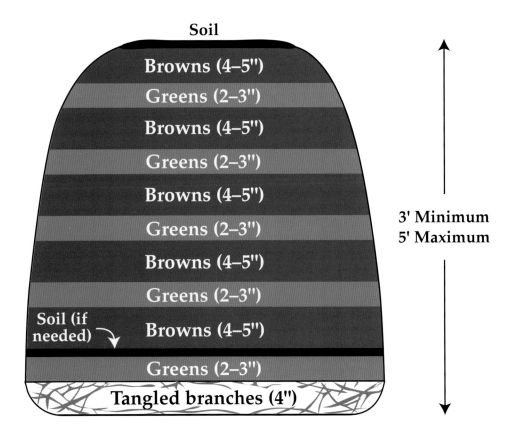

Soil

Browns (4–5")

Greens (2–3")

Browns (4–5")

Greens (2–3")

Browns (4–5")

Greens (2–3")

Browns (4–5")

Greens (2–3")

Soil (if needed) → Browns (4–5")

Greens (2–3")

Tangled branches (4")

3' Minimum
5' Maximum

Materials and tools

- ❑ Clippers or pruning shears

- ❑ Watering can and water

- ❑ Gloves

- ❑ Shovel or pitchfork

- ❑ Enough greens and browns to build a pile no smaller than 3 feet square, with alternating levels of each material added like a giant layer cake.

- ❑ Soil—if your material is fresh and has not decomposed at all, make sure you have a couple of handfuls available to add to the pile. Soil contains the microbes needed for decomposition.

Building the Pile

1. Gather your organic materials near the spot where you intend to build the pile.

2. Chop or shred large pieces of material to make them easier to be eaten by the microbes.

3. Water the ground liberally at the bottom of the bin to help the pile retain moisture.

4. Start the foundation of the pile with a 4-inch layer of bulky browns such as branches, twigs, and limbs.

5. Water these browns liberally. A full watering can most likely will be enough, except if the materials you are adding are extremely dry at the outset. Use your judgment.

7. Water this layer liberally.

This tangle of material will help keep the pile elevated and will allow air to flow upward into it.

6. Add a 2-inch layer of greens. Do not pack down the greens; let them settle naturally to create air pockets in the pile.

8. Add a few handfuls of soil. This will instantly increase the number of microbes in the pile, which will help speed up the composting process.

Take Note

Soil scientists have found that one teaspoon of healthy garden soil contains 100 million bacteria and 800 feet of fungal threads.

9. Continue by adding a 4–5-inch layer of browns.

10. Water thoroughly.

11. Add a 2–3-inch layer of greens.

12. Water thoroughly.

13. Repeat steps 9–12 until your pile has reached a height not less than 3 feet high but no greater than 5 feet high. At a height under 3 feet, decomposition will be inefficient and slow, perhaps taking more than a year to fully decompose; at a height greater than 5 feet, composting can progress too rapidly, creating bad odors and high levels of heat.

14. Top the pile with a final layer of browns, and add a few more handfuls of soil if necessary.

Water these last layers. Store excess materials for use later.

Take Note

Make sure that all food scraps are well buried in the pile to lessen the chances of attracting insects or four-legged pests.

Your pile has now begun to decompose. How quickly that process occurs rests in your hands. If you do nothing further to the pile at all, you will get a bin of finished compost in about a year or so. With a bit of work on your part, you can get finished compost in several months.

To accelerate the process, you must tend the pile to maintain a favorable environment for the microbes to do their work. The favorable environment, keep in mind, means a proper supply of water and air. You will know that the process is working by the heat generated inside the pile.

The material should have the moist feel of a wrung-out sponge—not dry, but not dripping with water either. If too wet, allow the compost to dry; if too dry, add water.

To periodically introduce air into the pile as it settles, use a pitchfork or shovel to turn the material over like tossing a giant salad. Make sure ingredients that have settled to the bottom are shuffled to the top, and that materials around the outer edge make it into the center of the pile.

Sometimes turning a pile built inside a commercial bin is tricky because of limited space for using a shovel or other tool.

A good solution is to simply lift the bin off the pile and set it down in a different location nearby.

Use a shovel or pitchfork to load the material back into the bin.

You can also use an aerating device to agitate the pile and introduce more oxygen without having to turn the whole heap. Aerators come in a variety of styles, but they all are designed to poke down into the pile and "fluff up" the material.

Sometimes the pile can become compacted in the center, so some force is required when pulling up on the tool.

Make sure you drive the device down into the pile at numerous spots to make sure most ingredients have been disturbed.

You will know this technique is working when darker, partially decomposed material rises to the surface.

As a general rule, turning or aerating the pile weekly and making sure it has the proper moisture content will produce finished compost within several months.

For a more hands-on approach, turn the pile on the second day after it is built, again on the fourth day, then every three days until the compost is finished. Some experts have managed to create usable compost in two weeks with this method!

A Matter of Time

No turning = Up to a year or more

Weekly turning = Several months

Frequent turning (every 3 days) = Several weeks

After a week or two, you will notice that the pile has shrunk noticeably. Material is breaking down and compacting on itself. When the pile is finished, its volume will have decreased dramatically, and the original weight of the material will have dropped by as much as 50 percent.

Take Note

As an alternative to single-batch composting, you can continuously add additional food scraps and other new material to the pile and turn it under as needed, as long as you maintain the general balance of carbon to nitrogen. Remember, not all of the compost will be ready at the same time using this method. The material at the bottom of the pile will turn to compost first.

If you smell the odor of vinegar or rotten eggs coming from your pile, anaerobic decomposition most likely is taking place. That means the pile either contains too much moisture or is compacted so tightly that no air can reach the interior. To correct this, turn the pile and add dry, porous material such as straw or wood chips to soak up the moisture.

If you smell a distinct odor of ammonia, your pile most likely contains too much nitrogen. Correct this by adding materials high in carbon, such as straw, sawdust, or wood chips.

If your pile doesn't seem to be heating up, there are a number of possible causes: the pile might be too small or too dry, or it might lack air or nitrogen. All of these deficiencies will slow decomposition dramatically. Correct the problem by increasing the size of the pile, adding water, adding greens, or turning it. In the opposite case, the pile might become too hot if it becomes too large—greater than 5 feet high—or lacks sufficient ventilation. Reduce the size of the pile or aerate it.

Temperatures at or below freezing will slow the composting process almost completely—making the cold winter months in many regions poor for fast composting.

A WORD ABOUT ACTIVATORS

Compost activators or inoculators are sold commercially and designed to be applied to a compost pile to accelerate the process. These activators are usually nitrogen-rich and contain live bacteria and enzymes. Most experts agree that there is no need to use them at all because nature will provide the correct amount and types of microorganisms needed for decomposition.

THE HIDDEN LIFE OF THE COMPOST PILE

As soon as you build the compost pile, microorganisms start consuming the organic materials. The microbes produce heat, water, and carbon dioxide as a by-product of the decomposition process.

This decomposition occurs in an organized sequence.

1. During the first stage of decomposition, microbes called **psychrophiles** arrive and go to work. They appear when the pile temperature is cool, from 55 to 70 degrees Fahrenheit (F). Once these bacteria start to digest the food, they release carbon dioxide, water, and heat as a by-product. The generation of heat by these microorganisms causes the compost pile temperature to rise, which attracts different bacteria.

2. Next to appear are the **mesophiles**. They thrive when temperatures in the pile reach from 70 to 90 degrees F. These bacteria perform most of the decomposition in your pile.

3. The next stage of decomposition comes with the arrival of microbes called **thermophiles**, when temperatures within the pile reach 104 degrees F and above. When temperatures in the pile become that hot, almost all weed seeds and harmful organisms are destroyed.

These stages or sequences and rise in temperature in the pile indicate the compost process is occurring properly. The compost pile will steadily lose heat after the thermophiles are finished eating their food source. The pile temperature

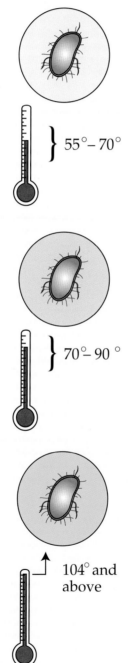

} 55°– 70°

} 70°– 90°

104° and above

will decrease, and the mesophiles will come back to the pile and keep eating.

Not all decomposition occurs at the microbiological level.

Small insects and other invertebrates—earthworms, millipedes, sow bugs, grubs, mites, snails, spiders, and nematodes—feed on the bacteria and fungi throughout the compost pile and help with decomposition. The presence of these organisms is a good indicator that the compost pile is healthy and decomposition is occurring. As they burrow through the compost pile in search of food, they help to mix the organic materials and create natural tunnels that provide air circulation throughout the pile.

The illustration on the following page shows the process by which organic materials are broken down. Initially, microorganisms, termed first-level decomposers, go to work. Second-level decomposers, such as small beetles and mites, are next to consume materials, followed by larger invertebrates known as third-level decomposers.

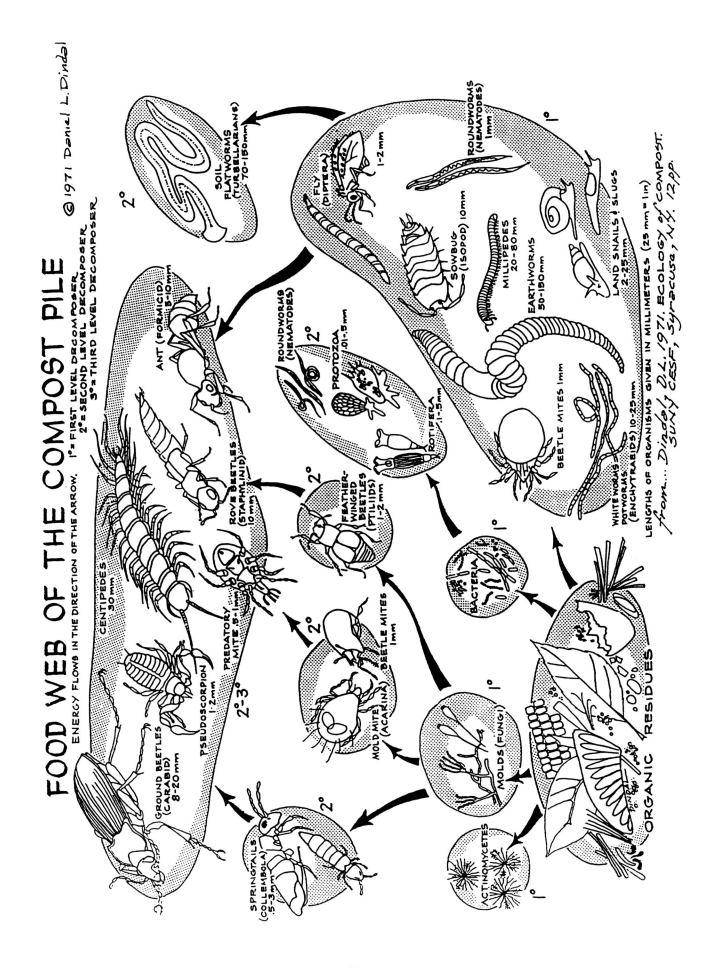

FOOD WEB OF THE COMPOST PILE

ENERGY FLOWS IN THE DIRECTION OF THE ARROW.
1° = FIRST LEVEL DECOMPOSER.
2° = SECOND LEVEL DECOMPOSER
3° = THIRD LEVEL DECOMPOSER

© 1971 Daniel L. Dindal

SOIL FLATWORMS (TURBELLARIANS) 70-150mm

2°

FLY (DIPTERA) 1-2mm

ROUNDWORMS (NEMATODES) 1mm

SOWBUG (ISOPOD) 10mm

MILLIPEDES 20-80mm

EARTHWORMS 50-150mm

LAND SNAILS & SLUGS 2-25mm

1°

BEETLE MITES 1mm

WHITE WORMS = POTWORMS (ENCHYTRAEIDS) 10-25mm

ANT (FORMICID) 5-10mm

ROUNDWORMS (NEMATODES)

2°

PROTOZOA .01-.5mm

ROTIFERA 1-5mm

CENTIPEDES 30mm

ROVE BEETLES (STAPHYLINID) 10mm

2°

FEATHER-WINGED BEETLES (PTILIIDS) 1-2mm

PSEUDOSCORPION 1-2mm

PREDATORY MITE .5-1mm

2°-3°

BACTERIA

1°

2°

MOLD MITE (ACARINA)

BEETLE MITES 1mm

MOLDS (FUNGI)

1°

GROUND BEETLES (CARABID) 8-20mm

SPRINGTAILS (COLLEMBOLA) .5-3mm

2°

ACTINOMYCETES

1°

ORGANIC RESIDUES

LENGTHS OF ORGANISMS GIVEN IN MILLIMETERS (25 mm = 1 in)

From... Dindal, D.L. 1971. Ecology of Compost.
SUNY CESF, Syracuse, N.Y. 12 pp.

47

Alternative Composting Methods: No Bin

Buried pile composting

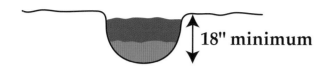

18" minimum

The method follows the same theory as a pile made in a bin, except that materials are placed into a pit in the ground. The pit should be no less than 18 inches deep and should have a circumference large enough to accommodate several square feet of material. This helps to contain the pile and shelters it, promoting the development of higher temperatures and faster decomposition. The buried pile can be covered with a blanket or tarp to help it retain even more heat and moisture, deter pests and vermin, and keep the materials contained. You must maintain this pile regularly, or anaerobic conditions might take over fairly rapidly because of poor ventilation.

Trench or sheet composting

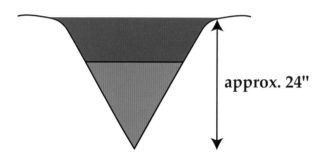

approx. 24"

This method is very similar to the buried pile technique, except that longer pits or trenches are dug in the ground. Trench composting is perfect for use in an area that you intend to till and convert into a vegetable or flower garden in the future.

Dig a trench roughly 2 feet deep and as long and as wide as you wish. The trench should span the length of the area you intend to use for your garden. Fill the hole with alternating layers of browns and greens and water liberally, as explained in the section on the proper technique for building a compost pile. When finished adding materials, cover the trench with a tarp or plastic sheets or with dirt removed from the trench.

Trench composting is generally a "fix it and forget it" kind of project. With that in mind, composting will take considerably longer than in a pile that is maintained regularly. Consider building the trench early in the spring and tilling late in the fall, or even wait a year for everything to decompose well in the ground.

When Compost Is Ready

Finished compost has a dark color much like coffee grounds and resembles thick, moist soil. It should have an earthy, fresh aroma and should not smell sour. No starting ingredients should be easily identified in finished compost; if you see fruit peels or the like, you should allow the compost to break down longer.

If you are still unsure about the status of your compost, try this simple test: Place a couple ounces of compost in a plastic bag with a seal, such as the type sold for storing food in the freezer. Make sure the bag is sealed and place it in the refrigerator for about 48 hours. If you smell no strong odors when the bag is opened, the compost is ready. Otherwise, a foul odor means too much organic matter remains intact and must be decomposed further. As explained earlier, noxious odors are produced when once-living material decomposes in an environment that provides little air, such as the conditions inside the sandwich bag.

7

Compost Screener

Y ou can use finished compost straight out of the bin, but a screener is handy if you want to eliminate larger chunks of material, sift the compost into a finer consistency, and separate finished compost from unfinished material.

The sifting process is easy.
Simply load several small piles of compost from the pile into the screener and agitate it until smaller pieces fall through the screen.

You can let the finer compost settle onto the ground or onto a tarp, or you can set the screen on a container or wheelbarrow to catch falling material. Use your hand or a small shovel to help rub the compost across the screen.

Remember to return larger hunks of wood and other organic debris back to the pile for further decomposition.

Materials

PINE BOARD
1 inch by 6 inches by 8 feet

SCREWS
Twelve 2-inch galvanized
deck screws and twenty-
four $1^5/8$-inch galvanized
deck screws.

MESH
$^1/2$-inch mesh cut to
18 inches by 24 inches.

Tools

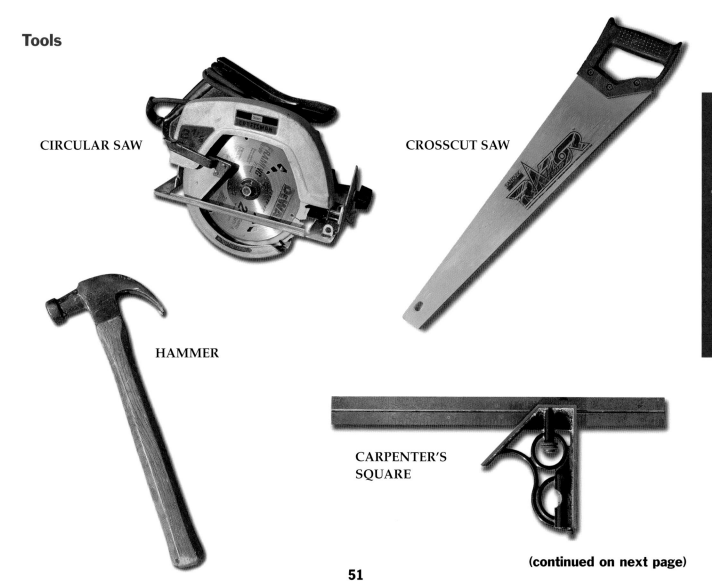

CIRCULAR SAW

CROSSCUT SAW

HAMMER

**CARPENTER'S
SQUARE**

Compost Screener

(continued on next page)

Tools (continued)

Compost Screener

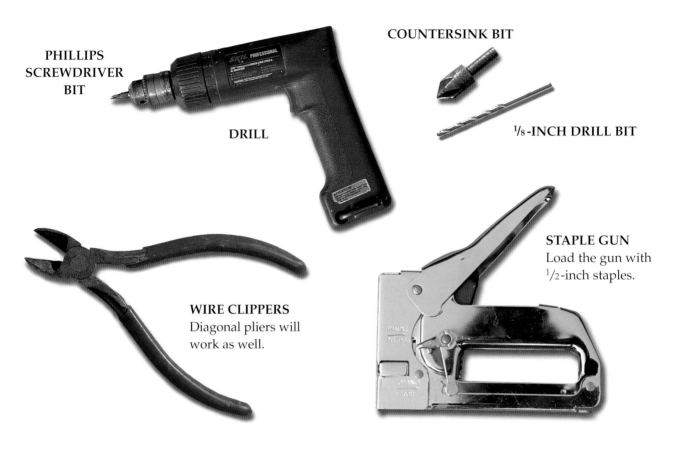

PHILLIPS
SCREWDRIVER
BIT

DRILL

COUNTERSINK BIT

¹/₈-INCH DRILL BIT

WIRE CLIPPERS
Diagonal pliers will
work as well.

STAPLE GUN
Load the gun with
¹/₂-inch staples.

SANDPAPER
For best results, use coarse paper on
a sanding block.

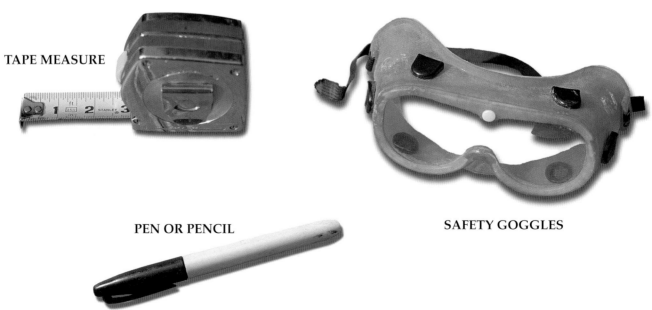

TAPE MEASURE

SAFETY GOGGLES

PEN OR PENCIL

Compost Screener

1. Roll out hardware cloth.

2. Measure and cut it to make a piece that measures 18 inches by 24 inches.

3. Measure two 1-inch by 6-inch boards $^1/_2$ inch greater than the length of the hardware cloth (about $24^1/_2$ inches).

4. Measure two 1-inch by 6-inch boards 1 inch less than the width of the hardware cloth (about 17 inches).

5. Measure a $^3/_8$-inch-thick strip of wood on the side of the 1- by 6-inch board.

6. The measured and marked plank should look like this.

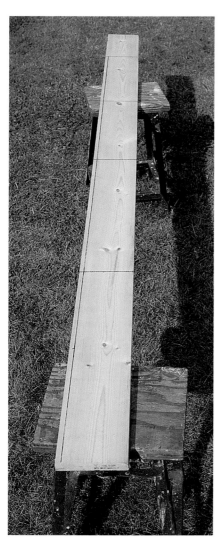

7. Cut the thin strip of wood from the board with a circular saw or handsaw.

Cut the long strip into four sections and set aside.

8. Cut the four larger boards.

9. Mark three holes for drilling $^3/_8$ inch from the ends of both of the 24$^1/_2$-inch boards, one at the center and two $^3/_4$ inch from each edge.

10. Drill the holes through the piece of wood.

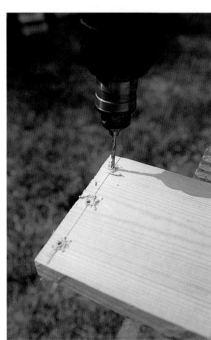

11. Mark holes for drilling $^3/_4$ inch from both ends of the four $^3/_8$-inch wood strips and approximately every 4 inches in between.

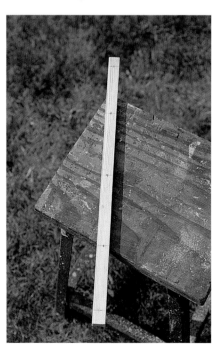

12. Drill a $1/8$-inch hole through each mark on the $24\frac{1}{2}$-inch boards and the $3/8$-inch wood strips.

13. Place countersink bit into drill.

Countersink each hole you drilled to a depth that will accept the head of the galvanized deck screws.

14. Begin assembly of the screen frame by aligning the edge of a $24\frac{1}{2}$-inch board with the end of a 17-inch board and inserting a $1\frac{5}{8}$-inch galvanized deck screw into each of the three holes.

15. Drive each screw into the hole until its head sits completely in the countersink hole.

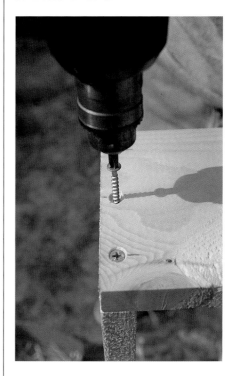

16. Repeat for each corner of the screen frame, creating a rectangular frame. You can use the right angle of the carpenter's square to test this.

17. Place the cut piece of hardware cloth onto the screen frame.

18. Staple the screen in place about every 3 inches along the perimeter of the frame.

Tap staples flush to the surface of the wood with the hammer if necessary.

19. Match the $^3/_8$-inch wood strips with their corresponding sides of the frame, align the strips with the edges and ends of the rectangle, and fasten each strip into place one at a time using $1^5/_8$-inch galvanized deck screws.

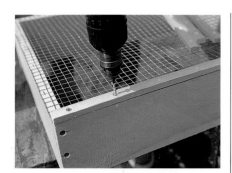

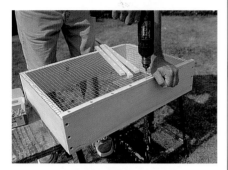

20. Use sandpaper to smooth the edges of the frame.

21. Test the screener by sifting 1 gallon of finished compost through the screen or as much as you are comfortable supporting if holding the screener.

Take Note

Do not overload the screener or attempt to sift wet compost.

8

Uses for Finished Compost

Properly created compost is among the best substances that can be added to the soil year-round. Unlike fertilizers, which must be used precisely and infrequently, compost can be applied virtually anywhere and at any time without risk of injuring or "burning" plants. When turned into the ground through tilling, compost can improve the condition of the soil by allowing it to hold more air and water.

At the same time, compost adds nutrients to make plants healthier and can protect plants from a variety of diseases commonly found in the garden.

The following information pertains to organic compost. Worm castings harvested from worm composting contain higher concentrations of nutrients than regular compost and should be used in slightly lower amounts.

In a new garden or flower bed

A layer about 4 inches thick may be tilled into the soil of the bed prior to planting. Freshly incorporated plants will enjoy the benefits of compost's fertility, disease protection, erosion control, and drought resistance. When starting plants from seeds or small first growths, make sure to use finished compost. Avoid using compost that contains obvious pieces of organic matter that has not decomposed—this material is not ready to be used on tender vegetation because it can retard proper growth or spread undigested weed seeds or plant disease.

Annuals, flowers, and vegetables alike can remain healthy and vibrant through the use of compost as well; till it into the soil prior to planting or add it afterward. To do that, simply spread a thin layer of the material around the base of the plants; rain will help the nutrients work into the soil—and, by extension, into the roots of the plants—over time. If your gardens have been mulched, it's necessary to push it aside before adding the compost, and then spread the mulch back into place once finished. This technique also works well for perennials in the springtime and when they appear to need a boost.

On the lawn

Finished compost spread to a depth of $1/4$ inch over a newly seeded lawn will help the young grass take root and thrive. Mature lawns will stay healthy with an application.

Finished compost can be added to bare spots on a lawn to improve soil quality over time. Just spread densely and let nature go to work.

In small containers or pots

Mix regular soil with finished, screened compost to create your own potting mix for houseplants or to start new plants from seeds. No more than one-third of the mixture should be compost, to allow roots to take hold firmly.

It is very important to use only finished compost with seeds and tender transplants, because some toxins or other substances harmful to plants might remain from incomplete decomposition. Don't pot plants in compost alone, because the roots need a coarser substance such as soil to grip firmly.

Uses for Finished Compost

63

As mulch

Use compost that is not quite finished and still has larger chunks of wood and organic debris present. These larger pieces will continue to decompose once they are spread as mulch in garden and flower beds and around the bases of trees. Because compost should be thick and heavy for use as mulch, do not screen the compost first.

Take Note

Certain plants do not respond well to increased releases of nitrogen that can spread from unfinished compost used as mulch. The best rule of thumb is to monitor the health of plant life following an application of mulch and react accordingly based on results.

Around trees

Spread a layer 2 to 4 inches thick around the roots to provide nutrients and to protect mature or newly planted trees from drought and disease. This also helps to suppress weed growth. Apply the compost once or twice a year, depending on how well the tree appears to be growing.

FROM THE EXPERTS

Compost works well in moderate amounts around the garden or vegetable patch. That means there is no need for you to smother topsoil with large amounts of it. A good rule of thumb is to apply about 2 inches of compost on top of the soil before tilling or as mulch. In areas subject to prolonged periods of heat or dryness, increase the amount of compost you apply by an inch or two; this will help the soil to stay moist when little precipitation falls. In moist areas prone to soggy rainy seasons, several layers of compost can help absorb excess runoff and keep plant roots from rotting.

Take Note

Do not use compost alone in the bottom of hole dug for a new planting of a tree of shrub; the moisture-holding characteristics of compost could prevent the fresh roots from seeking out new sources of nutrients and water in the surrounding soil. Instead, mix the compost with some soil.

9

Compost Tea

True to its name, compost tea is a brownish, translucent liquid that can easily be made by soaking or steeping finished compost in water. The tea contains concentrations of nutrients and beneficial organisms that will increase plant growth and health and help suppress diseases. The tea also will eliminate the need to use toxic, store-bought chemicals in your garden such as fertilizers, pesticides, and fungicides. The liquid is typically sprayed onto the leaves of the plants or applied to the soil and roots with a watering can.

There are two common ways to "brew" your own compost tea. The first method takes some effort to set up and complete, but the finished tea produced is superior to any other method. An aerator pump like the kind found in an aquarium is used to circulate air throughout a mixture of water and finished compost. This additional oxygen in the mixture allows an incredible amount of beneficial microorganisms to grow.

The second method does not use aeration. It is the easiest and quickest way to make beneficial tea, but it will not have the same quality as the first method.

Method One (Aerated)

Materials and tools

COMPOST
Have at least one gallon on hand.

BUCKETS
You'll need two 5-gallon containers.

AERATOR PUMP
A pump like that found on an aquarium will work fine.

WATER
4 gallons' worth—bottled water or rainwater is recommended because it does not contain chlorine, which can kill off some of the valuable microorganisms.

"GANG" VALVE
Use a three- or four-channel valve to connect the pump to the water and compost.

AQUARIUM HOSE
One 4-foot length.

CHEESECLOTH
Find a section measuring at least 3 feet by 3 feet

CLOTHESPINS

LONG SPOON
For stirring—you can also just use a stick or your hand.

WATERING CAN

Take Note
You likely will also need an outdoor extension cord and a power source to run the aerator for about three days. This project can get a little messy, so it is best to complete it outdoors.

Compost Tea

1. Gather equipment and materials.

2. Add enough compost to fill a 5-gallon bucket halfway.

3. Add enough water to fill the bucket to within several inches of the rim.

4. Hang the gang valve on the edge of the bucket.

5. Place the aerator pump on the ground and measure a length of plastic tubing between it and the gang valve.

6. Cut the hose to the correct length.

7. Attach the hose to the outflow nozzle on the aerator pump and

to the main intake fitting on the gang valve.

8. Measure a length of hose that will reach from the gang valve to the bottom of the bucket.

9. Cut this section of hose.

10. Use this section as a measurement guide and cut three additional pieces of hose the same length.

11. Attach the hoses to the gang valve.

14. Let the mixture "brew" and percolate for two to three days, enabling the organisms to multiply while the swirling water extracts nutrients from the finished compost. You can stir the mixture once a day to keep things mixed well and to help separate the microorganisms from the pieces of compost.

12. Submerge the hoses in the water, making sure they extend down to the bottom of the bucket.

15. After the tea has brewed, turn off the pump, remove the hoses, and check the mixture for rancid odors. The tea should smell sweet and earthy. If it smells like rotten eggs or spoiled food, do not use it on your plants. Too much anaerobic decomposition has occurred, probably because the source compost was not mature enough. Simply dump the entire mixture back into the compost pile and wait for fully finished material.

If the contents of the bucket smell earthy, they are ready to be strained.

13. Make sure the airflow valves are open, and activate the pump.

16. Cut a section of cheesecloth and place it over the second empty bucket.

17. Secure it to the bucket with clothespins.

18. Pour the mixture onto the cheesecloth.

19. The cloth will catch larger pieces of compost and allow the liquid to pass through; be sure to return the large chunks back to your compost pile.

20. The compost tea can be strained a second time to eliminate even more sediment if desired.

21. Transfer the compost liquid into a watering can. It is best to use the tea immediately because the beneficial microorganisms will begin to die off once the flowing air from the aquarium pump is removed.

22. Apply the tea to plants as you would regular water. The tea will give plants a boost of nutrients and energy for improved heartiness. You can apply compost tea to your plants and garden every two to three weeks.

Method Two (Non-Aerated)

Fill a large bucket or similar container about halfway with water.

Add finished compost until the water level is several inches lower than the rim.

Stir the mixture well.

Let the compost soak for two to three days, stirring once each day.

Use cheesecloth stretched over a second bucket to separate the debris from the liquid.

The compost tea will be dark brown and loaded with plant nutrients. After the tea has brewed, check it for rancid odors. The tea should smell sweet and earthy. If it smells like rotten eggs or spoiled food, do not use it on your plants. Put it back in the compost pile and wait for it to decompose further.

Strain larger chunks from the tea, transfer it to a watering can or similar container, and apply it to plants every two to three weeks as you would regular water.

10
Worm Composting

As the name suggests, this type of composting relies on hungry worms in bins to break down organic food scraps and bedding material into a very nutrient-rich fertilizer for plants. As the worms munch on the leftover food you provide for them, they convert it into a waste product called castings.

Castings contain even more nutrients than conventional compost, making them the perfect addition to any potted plant, garden, or window box.

Worm castings are moist and dark brown or black like coffee grounds.

Despite the conventional wisdom that worms are dirty and germ-ridden, worm composting is sanitary, odorless, and very efficient if done properly. Those traits make it perfect for both indoor and outdoor settings.

The key to the whole process is the hearty and hungry redworm, known to anglers as the "red wiggler," or the smaller but equally ravenous brown-nose worm, known as the "manure worm." A pound of these worms can devour about a pound of food scraps and bedding in about a week, given the correct environment. They reproduce quickly under favorable conditions, doubling their population once every three months or so. This means that an initial batch of worms, properly maintained, will produce good compost indefinitely.

The digestive tract inside a worm, which stretches much of its length, uses enzymes excreted by both the worm's intestines and by bacteria to break down organic materials. At the same time, minerals and other substances are broken down into usable form for plants, carbon dioxide is released into the air, and sugars are broken down. All of this material is expelled from the worm's anus in the form of moist casings.

Earthworms such as nightcrawlers must not be used for this type of composting; they require large amounts of soil to survive and will die in bins loaded with food scraps.

Redworms and manure worms—scientific names *Lumbricus rubellus* and *Eisenia foetida*—are relatively small, and large numbers of them can fit into a small area. For instance, hundreds of mature worms easily can occupy 1 square foot of space. This attribute makes them the perfect choice for apartment dwellers or city residents who want to compost but don't have access to land. A plastic or rubber container and lid measuring just 12 inches long, 10 inches wide, and 10 inches high will do the trick. Redworms dislike sunlight, so make sure the container is opaque and doesn't let in any light.

Above: The redworm, Lumbricus rubellus. *Right: The manure worm,* Eisenia foetida.

If you can't find a bait shop in your area, simply type "worm" + "wholesale" into your favorite search engine to find online suppliers. Keep in mind that earthworms must not be used for vermicomposting; they require large amounts of soil to live and will perish inside the composting container.

Search the Web

"worm"+"wholesale"   Search

It can be stored under the sink or in any out-of-the-way place, or it can be placed outside just like a regular composting bin. Larger bins that hold more worms and food waste can be set up as space allows.

Instructions on building a plastic worm bin for indoor or outdoor use are provided in this section.

Take Note

Keep in mind that temperature extremes can be deadly to worms. Indoors, temperatures can be controlled easily. Outdoors, though, worms in plastic bins need to be monitored to protect them from temperatures above 80 degrees or below 50 degrees. During overly warm or cold periods, take the bins inside.

An alternative to the plastic bin is a permanent outdoor one made of cinder blocks, much like the one used for traditional composting shown on page 21. This type of container is best suited for use in areas where the climate is moderate year-round. Because the floor of the permanent bin is earth, redworms will burrow into the ground to escape temperature extremes. However, the worms will have a difficult time surviving during prolonged, harsh winters, such as the kind found in the Northeast and Midwest sections of the United States.

The instructions for building a cinder block bin must be modified when making a worm bin. Instead of leaving the front of the bin open, place at least two rows of blocks across the opening to help corral the worms.

Materials

PLASTIC BIN

These storage containers, which are available in 5- to 10-gallon sizes, are available in home improvement and department stores. Make sure the container has a lid that fits well; this will deter pets and other animals if the bin is placed outdoors.

PAPER

Worms need moistened, shredded bedding material to provide an ancillary food source and to provide a beneficial environment. Newspaper or plain paper will work fine, as will shredded cardboard, fallen leaves, sawdust, and dried grass clippings.

    You will need enough moist paper to fill half the bin. Avoid using paper that contains colored ink, because it might contain substances toxic to the worms. Black ink will create no problems. Do not use glossy paper—the kind used in magazines and newspaper inserts—because of toxicity and digestion issues.

FOOD SCRAPS

The worms will devour much of the leftovers a family generates, such as fruit and vegetable peels, egg shells, tea bags, coffee grounds, and similar items. As with a traditional compost bin, avoid adding meats or dairy products to the worm bin to cut down on odors and problems with pests. Use care when adding citrus fruits, because excessive acid content might hurt the worms.

WORMS

Redworms and manure worms are recommended for worm composting. They can be found in many bait shops and generally cost $2 to $3 per dozen; depending on the size of the worms, ten to fifteen dozen worms may be needed to equal a pound. Keep the worms in the refrigerator—not the freezer—until you are ready to use them. They will be sluggish at first until they warm up to room temperature.

77

DRILL, DRILL BIT
Use to create a series of air holes several inches above the mid-point of the bin. Worms, like all living things, must have an unobstructed source of oxygen to survive. A regular $1/4$- to $1/2$-inch drill bit will work fine, but a drywall bit with a sharpened tip will penetrate the bin more quickly.

EXTENSION CORD
Use with the drill or paper shredder if needed.

PAPER SHREDDER
Makes short work of chopping and shredding the paper needed for worm bedding.

LARGE BOWL
Fill with water and use to soak the paper needed for worm bedding.

CUTTING BOARD, KNIFE
You can chop large pieces of food into smaller bits to help the worms do their job more quickly.

Worm Composting Bin

Worms, like all living things, need air to survive. Because most store-bought storage bins are of solid construction, you likely will have to drill holes in yours for ventilation.

1. Place the bin on a flat, level surface for support.

2. Choose a side and drill a hole about 3 inches from the top edge of the bin.

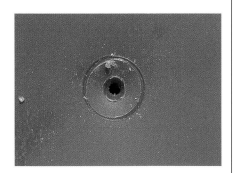

3. Continue around the perimeter, drilling holes about 1$\frac{1}{2}$ inches apart.

4. When finished, empty the bin of any plastic shavings or plugs left by drilling.

5. Rip newspaper pages into small pieces by hand or use a paper shredder to get the job done quickly. Paper strips should be no more than an inch or two wide; they shouldn't be shredded as fine as confetti, either.

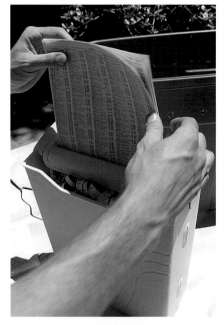

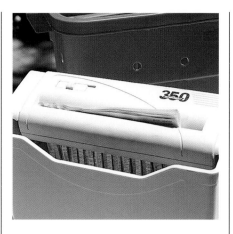

6. Once the shredding is completed, fill a large pot or bucket with water. You may want to work over a sink or outside.

7. Take a pile of the paper and dip it in the water. It will become saturated in a matter of seconds.

8. Remove the wet paper from the bucket and squeeze out most of the water. The paper must be wet without being soggy or dripping; otherwise, the container will collect stagnant water that could produce bad odors and harm the worms. By the same token, don't squeeze every last drop of moisture out either. Pick a point somewhere in the middle; the feel should be that of a partially wrung-out sponge.

11. Continue dipping, soaking, squeezing, and peeling the paper until the bin is about half full. Do not pack the paper down; it needs to just settle on its own so the worms, when added, can burrow without resistance.

9. Squeezing will make the paper form into a tight wad, so you need to loosen it and pull the paper apart.

10. Place these pieces into the bottom of the bin.

81

Once the bedding is in place, it's time to add the worms. If you are squeamish about handling them, use rubber dishwashing gloves or latex surgical gloves sold in the drug store.

Redworms are pretty tough, but you should still use a gentle touch when handling them.

Reach down into the bedding and lift up a section to get to a lower layer. Place a handful of worms in that area. Worms hate bright lights and naturally seek out dark spaces, so recently added worms will seem to vanish into thin air. Don't add worms directly on top of the bedding—they'll have to work harder to get to the bottom, and some may be too lethargic from the cold storage to make it. Repeat the process at different spots in the bin until the worms all have been used.

Worms prefer a weekly diet of vegetables and fruit scraps, but they also will eat bread, coffee grounds and paper filters, and crushed egg shells—not the yolks, though. In fact, egg shells or a little bit of coarse sand or soil must be added from time to time—once every month or two—to aid in the worms' digestive process. A pound of food scraps should be added every seven to ten days for every pound of worms; don't go longer than a month without adding food scraps.

Although some worms may eat everything in sight, others may avoid particular kinds of foods, such as onions or broccoli. It's always a good idea to check their eating habits every week or ten days; simply remove items that the worms seem to be ignoring before they begin fermenting and giving off rank aromas.

Worms will eat whole fruits and uncut vegetables over time, but chopping the food to smaller bits before feeding speeds up the process.

During feedings, carefully bury the food scraps down in the bedding. Worms tend to eat in layers, beginning with the food at the bottom. As that is consumed, they move upward to find more. Don't place the scraps on top of the bedding; the bin will produce rank odors in no time, possibly attracting insects, vermin, and other pests. One common pest is the fruitfly, which is harmless to both humans and worms but which can be an annoyance. To reduce the risk of fruitflies, you should make sure food scraps are buried under paper after each feeding.

FROM THE EXPERTS

Use a large plastic butter or ice cream container to store food scraps in your refrigerator until it's time to feed your worms. This will keep the food from spoiling too quickly and causing odor problems.

Worm Composting

Worm Composting

Check the moisture content of the bedding every time you add food scraps. If the bedding seems to be drying too much, add a little more water with a spray bottle or watering can. Do not oversaturate. If liquid appears to be collecting in the bottom of the bin, add more strips of paper to absorb it. Some experts prefer to drill holes in the bottom of the bin to drain liquid that accumulates. However, this is a messy prospect that attracts unwanted visitors. Adding extra shredded paper when warranted solves the problem quickly and easily.

If unpleasant odors develop, the bedding might be packed together too tightly and material might be rotting. Mix the bedding around and fluff it up to reintroduce some air into it. If the problem persists, the composition of the bedding and materials might have become too acidic, which is usually caused by adding too much citrus fruit. Correct this by adding a spoonful or two of powdered limestone. A little should work fine.

Take Note

Do not add slaked or hydrated lime, because it will kill the worms.

Some worm composters say that worms have been known to try to escape from the container for unexplained reasons, usually by crawling up the sides and out the air holes. It's a rare event, but one that bears watching. Most likely, something in the worms' environment has become unsatisfactory to them. Check food supply, moisture level, acid content, temperature, and light issues to correct the problem.

As the worms continue to feed over the course of several months, the level of the bedding will drop noticeably and the paper will darken. Add more moistened paper as warranted. During warm months, make sure the container is placed in a shaded area. In direct sunlight, temperatures inside the bin may increase to a level detrimental to the worms.

Castings look like dark, rich coffee grounds. They should be collected from the bin once every three months or so, or when most of the bedding material has disappeared. This gives you some fertilizer to add to your plants, and it gives the worms more room to move. In some instances, high concentrations of castings can become toxic to the worms.

It's easiest to remove the castings when the worms have reduced the bedding to a low level, so there is less material to deal with.

Use the worms' natural aversion to bright light to help in harvesting. To do this, take the bin outside into full sunlight and remove the lid. You may want to don gloves at this point, but it is not mandatory. Wait a couple of minute and remove the top layer of bedding—if there is any.

Use a small shovel, rake, or your hand to pull castings toward you. Keep your eye out for any stray worms that may have been removed along with the castings and excess bedding.

Pull large hunks of paper from the castings and return these pieces of paper to the bin for further composting.

Put the worms back in the bin or a separate container until the harvesting is finished.

Place the castings in a separate container. Return any uneaten scraps back into the bin.

Wait a couple more minutes or until no worms are visible on the surface. Once they have burrowed more deeply, again remove the top several inches of material and separate worms, castings, and uneaten materials.

Continue until the castings have been removed, then refill the bin with moist strips of paper and add food scraps.

Worm Composting

Alternative Methods

Instead of using direct sunlight, use a bright light such as a gooseneck lamp to drive the worms lower in the bin. This method allows you to harvest castings inside at any time.

Some worm composting experts use a fine screen to separate castings from worms and uneaten food scraps. Place small amounts of material on the screen to make sifting easier. Use a separate pan or container underneath the screen to catch the castings. Remember to use a very gentle side-to-side motion when straining materials so you don't injure the worms. Place any worms, larger pieces of bedding, or food items back into the worm bin.

Uses for Worm Castings

Once mixed with regular soil, the castings you have harvested can be used exactly like potting soil for container gardening or as fertilizer that can be applied in flower beds or vegetable gardens. Use about a teaspoon of castings for each cup of soil. The nutritious castings will produce lush, healthy plants and can spur very fast growth in seeds and young plants.

Resources

BOOKS ABOUT COMPOSTING

The following titles contain information and ideas useful to beginners looking to advance their skills or learn more technical aspects of composting.

Alexander, Ron. *Field Guide to Compost Use.* Harrisburg, PA. U.S. Composting Council, 1996.

Appelhof, Mary. *Worms Eat My Garbage.* Kalamazoo, MI: Flower Press, 1982.

Compost: Rodale Organic Gardening Basics Volume 8. Editors of Rodale Organic Gardening Magazine and Books. Emmaus, PA: Rodale Inc., 2001.

Roulac, John W. *Backyard Composting: Your Complete Guide to Recycling Yard Clippings.* Sebastopol, CA: Harmonious Technologies, 1997.

Stell, Elizabeth P. *Secrets of Great Soil.* Pownal, VT: Storey Communications, 1998.

ON THE INTERNET

www.mastercomposter.com
A great source for composting information, tips, and equipment advice.

www.dep.state.pa.us
This Web site for the Pennsylvania Department of Environmental Protection contains a good amount of information that home composters should find useful—including techniques and material on recycling.

www.a-horizon.com/compost/index2.htm
The Rot Web site, maintained by Eric S. Johnson, contains a copious amount of material pertaining to all skill levels of composting. Loaded with good details and tips.

www.oldgrowth.org/compost
This is the Composting Resource Page, loaded with details about small- and large-scale composting operations, products and services, and other information. Great site.